BIOGRAPHY OF
JULIE VON BARTMANN

BOOKS BY DJUNA BARNES
Published by Green Integer,
formerly Sun & Moon

POETRY
The Book of Repulsive Women

NONFICTION
Interviews
New York

ART
Poe's Mother: Selected Drawings

FICTION
Smoke and Other Early Stories

DRAMA
The Antiphon
At the Roots of the Stars: The Short Plays
Biography of Julie von Bartmann

BIOGRAPHY OF
Julie von Bartmann

Djuna Barnes

Introduction by Douglas Messerli

GREEN INTEGER
KØBENHAVN & LOS ANGELES
2020

GREEN INTEGER
Edited by Per Bregne
København / Los Angeles
(323) 937-3783 / www.greeninteger.com

Distributed in the United States by
Consortium Book Sales & Distribution / Ingram Books
(800) 283-3572 / www.cbsd.com

First Green Integer Edition 2020
Copyright ©2020 by Djuna Barnes
Back cover copy ©2020 by Green Integer
All rights reserved

Book Design: Pablo Capra
Cover photograph: Djuna Barnes

LIBRARY OF CONGRESS CATALOGING-IN-PUBLICATION DATA
Djuna Barnes [1892-1982]
Biography of Julie von Bartmann
ISBN: 978-1-55713-421-9
p. cm – Green Integer 211
I. Title II. Series

Green Integer books are published for Douglas Messerli
Printed in the USA

Table of Contents

Introduction: Freeing the Family

DOUGLAS MESSERLI

Written in Cagnes sur Mer in the Maritimes Alps in France between November 1923 and April 1924, Djuna Barnes' three-act play, *Biography of Julie von Bartmann*, is related to several of her early stories—particularly "A Night Among the Horses"—and to her 1928 fiction *Ryder*. Like the father, Wendell, of her fiction, the father of this early play, Basil Born, refuses to let his children attend public school, and challenges the school authorities, opposing their teaching methodologies: he wins. And like the early short story, one of Barnes' best, a strong and sophisticated woman verbally destroys her "bestial" horse groom.

Yet it is hard even to speak of "events" such as these in Barnes' work. Unlike most US plays, which lay out a "story" through their characters' lives, Barnes' highly artificed theater is centered in what one might describe as "revelations," mostly long statements about oneself and life, alternating with questions or sparring conversations, such as those between the powerful opera singer Julie von Bartmann and the strong-minded "landholder" Born. And even the "revelations" are less revealing of how the characters think than of how they perceive the world morally and philosophically. Since these statements are presented in a highly literary language, filled with aphorisms, puns, extended metaphors, and dualities, we cannot even be sure whether the character is speaking honestly or attempting to play out a desired notion of themselves.

Barnes begins the play in simple anticipation as Born's two sons, Gart and Costa (like her language, Barnes generally stocks her works with strangely named figures; not unlike her own name and those of her real-life brothers), await the arrival of their father and a new boarder, Julie, who is apparently staying at the house—the boys do some farming, but Born seems to have retired to rest up. Evidently, she is not the first grand person to stay with them; women, throughout the years, have had passionate relations with their father, even while their mother was still living.

Gart, the elder son, is thin and handsome, a gentle soul who plays the organ well. The younger son, Costa, is shorter and more broad-shouldered, a figure described as a kind of "beast," and having a connection with the soil. The daughter, Gustava, 19 years of age, is an excitable young woman who cares for pigeons and the garden. All three are in awe of their dominating father.

The rest of the drama plays out various encounters between these figures, in which each falls in love, in some respect, with the grand Julie. The first such "encounter" is understandably between Basil Born and Julie, and she questions him about himself, his children, and the house in which she is to stay. These passages, in particular, have the feel of a tennis match as each of these strong figures sends out charged and even barbed messages about their temperaments and sexualities:

> JULIE: I am not married, that is—not married. I have not money worries. I love—peculiarity, perhaps you would call it vice (*she raises her eyes watching him*). Nothing astonishes me. In the night, when it rains, when the lightning flashes and the thunder rolls, I do no not draw my toes up, I sleep, and leave terror and superstition to the people.
>
> BASIL: At a pinch madame, I can be a little peculiar myself.
>
> JULIE: It begins to be something of which I am aware. I have heard that you are savage. Is it so?
>
> BASIL: Not at all. I have a certain influence with my family, but the state does not like me.

At this point, he goes on to explain his encounters with "peoples in places of dictatorship" (i.e. the local school board). But the passage also clearly suggests Basil's interest in her, and she in him. The act ends indeed in a kind a *double entendre* as Julie says, "I am willing you should play a little," suggesting that she might hear him play a hymn upon the organ they have at their home; but with the end of that sentence, "but—I am noted for my detours!" she hints that the "playing" and "organ" might mean something else. Basil's command to his daughter, "Show that splendor to bed!" makes his desires, if not intentions, quite clear.

In the second scene of Act I, it is not Basil who visits Julie's bed, but Gustava, who snuggles up to Julie before pouring out a biography of the woman she has been following for years in fan magazines. Indeed, in another moment of the play, she is seen cutting out a picture from a magazine, several of which are posted on the Born walls. The vision she has of the grand lady is almost an inhuman one:

Wait, don't laugh. It is like this: You were born. You were laid in a bassinet, you did not cry. You learned to walk before other children, you watched everything, and then one day, when you were three or four, you realized that you were terrible, a child of destiny.

As Julie quickly perceives, Gustava is not quite the simple country girl she appears to be, soon moving even closer to the beautiful woman: "Let me put my head on your arm, your perfume is so strong, and so sweet." And by the end of their long conversation, she has hinted that Julie must come to terms with her—and her brothers—with Julie suggesting, "I have never reckoned with children," and Gustava responding, "Now you have come to it, we are here, what are you going to do?" Julie sends her away.

The second act begins with an extended conversation between Gustava and Costa, in which she recounts Julie's morning activities, both admitting their admiration for her ("She is beautiful"). When, soon after, Julie approaches Gart in an attempt to lure the seemingly shy 20-year-old out by describing her own past selves, Costa ends their conversation by striking his brother, the two of them violently wrestling while Julie looks on, clearly recognizing the emotional chaos she has created in them: "It has begun."

In the second scene of Act II, Barnes again creates a strangely ambiguous sexual scene, wherein Gart, troubled and unable to sleep, crawls into his father's bed, querying him about the dazzling visitor in their house

("Is Julie von Bartmann a good woman?" "Beautiful, damaged, therefore more beautiful," finally moving to his own perceived condition, "What is passion in man?").

The father, strongly demeaning Julie, is quite obviously, as he puts it, "trying to make Gart safe for tragedy." Nothing, however, can calm the excited young man, who almost dares his father to kill him ("No, you must finish my life. You have begun it and you must see it through.") before he threatens either suicide or murder: "I have come to something that I do not understand, or only in one way, I think it would not be your way.... Whether I must kill myself, or you."

There is only one way this tragedy can now play out. For the first time in the elder Born's life, he has meant less to a woman than his now nearly-grown children. At the age of 50, time has changed everything. When Born demands she choose him, what he describes as demanding "victory," she fends off his invitation to his bed, ultimately proclaiming she prefers "the shy, gentle elder son, half musician, half human."

By the end of the play, Born falls to the floor—as in *Nightwood*—becoming almost a dog before the towering Julie, while Gustava demands the intruder leave:

Go, go, it is all over. You see what he has managed—accomplished. Go, go, take everything and go. You see yourself—we are reunited—we need nothing—it is all finished—settled.

Upon leaving, Julie's slightly inexplicable reply, "Immense! Immense!" seems to suggest she perceives Born's act as a sort of sacrifice, an attempt to keep his family as a tightly knit unit opposed to the ridiculousness of others' lives. Yet one can only wonder if his act is not also a highly selfish one, the act of, as he describes himself, the Beast, desperate to hold onto what he has created in his insufferable pride.

Barnes does not answer the question, but surely we recognize the father's abandonment of his humanist pride to be a kind of bestial admiration of Julie, which closes both his and his family's biography, freeing these isolated orphans to enter the new world, to now lead their own lives, even if they are slightly wary of the foolishness that may face them. And in that sense, Barnes' theatrical family drama ends, much like Chekhov's plays, with a somewhat comedic, rather than tragic, resolution.

LOS ANGELES, JANUARY 15, 2013
Reprinted from *USTheater, Opera, and Performance*

BIOGRAPHY OF
Julie von Bartmann

PERSONS

MME. JULIE VON BARTMANN, prima donna, 38

BASIL BORN, landholder, 50

GART BORN, his eldest son, 20

GUSTAVA BORN, his daughter, next in age, 19

COSTA BORN, his youngest son, 18

Act First

SCENE FIRST

The BORN *farm.*
Time: late afternoon. October.

The general room.

While the room is primitive in comfort, nonexistent as a place of ease, it is nevertheless far from the ordinary type of farm interior. The beamed ceiling is pegged in wood, the walls are rough plaster, the floors substantial and stained dark. A stove, commonly known as a "station masters stove," burns to the left, near steps leading to the upper floor, the pipe running up into an upper chamber for the heat it carries. Before the stove there is a wide-armed chair with cushions. A square table stands centre right, and surrounding it are two stools and four chairs. Backstage left stands a foot organ. Back of the organ, though not covered by it, are two long windows looking out upon a stretch of field and beyond that, woods. The walls are covered with pictures evidently cut from colored supplements and pasted together without regard for period. Father Knickerbocker stands in ruffled silk coat and satin breeches, behind a lady with a parasol of the early seventies, a feather boa falling loosely over her full bust, to the hem of her pleated skirt, the head surmounted by a large leghorn hat, heavy with saxe blue plumes. Yet another, of a little prince in a lace collar regarding Leda with the swan. Three oak framed photogravures, obviously the Christmas plate of some musical magazine, hang between the windows, Liszt, Beethoven and Chopin. A large mirror between.

GART BORN is seated at the organ. He is a tall, lanky youth, with a shock of black hair, a long thin, bright face and quick clumsy movements. There is the skin, the coloring, the grossness of the country boy about him, but with a very personal seasoning. He wears heavy boots, a blue shirt and corduroy trousers. His hands, work-hardened and large, are quick upon the keys.

COSTA BORN, his younger brother, is seated on a bench. He is small, heavily built, with a round hard head and bright grey eyes. When he moves, when he speaks, there is something of the pugilist about him. He is dressed like his brother. He sits bent forward, his hands folded, one over the other, between his knees. Now and again he puts wood on the fire.

GART: *(Playing)* Father has too much passion.

COSTA: *(Gruffly, with the voice of a child breaking into manhood)* Why?

GART: Listen. He wants this played loud, thumping, crash of the hands. *(He plays loudly)* Bring your whole arm down. Perhaps it's because he is getting old, I don't know. See, I should like it like this *(He plays softly)* but no, he says one's technique must be heavy, like a bull's, for the concert hall, so that all the ladies, to the last row, can quiver. So I, Gart Born, dutiful son, play boom! boom! boom! and the ladies shall have what can be got out of them. *(He drops into a gentle waltz)*

COSTA: Uum.

GART: Personally I should think this would do more for a woman. *(He sways a little as he plays, his technique becoming almost Viennese)* So! *(He closes his eyes and begins as if quoting)* A kiss where she trembles most. A hand upon her bosom. Her gorge rises. "Life was so terrible Basil, when I was young. Cows calved, the bodkin ran like mad, and every buskin went back and forth in the pains of labour, but now, now I have known you, a strumpet gathers light feet at forty and thanks the Lord God for you between one thing and another."

COSTA: *(Grinning)* Who said that?

GART: Elsa, the thin, tall Elsa, she had smouldering passions, my brother, she was a tiger between tea and eventide. She rejoiced in Dad and demanded a war piece. *(He plays a war song)* Men, as strong as butchers, as tender as women, going down into war. Blare of the trumpet, there you are, vive your country, whatever it happened to be, annihilation in a foreign land, if possible for colour, a last-charge! A ditch taken, oblivion! "I love military pieces," she says, "with my meals it fills me with a beautiful terror."

COSTA: She arrives to-day.

GART: Who?

COSTA: That singing woman, what's her name.

GART: *(Glibly)* Mme. Julie von Bartmann—opera singer.

COSTA: Well, Julie von Bartmann. What in hell does she want on a farm?

GART: She comes, she recovers, it's simple.

COSTA: Recovers from what?

GART: Beauty, my little idiot, Thaïs, Salome, Luise. And for that there is nothing like the country. Long stretches of land between her and the singing season. Acres and acres that you don't have to think about. Simple people, but—there is Man Born. Dad has put many a woman back into the destiny of a nation. Remember Della, she of the long bright braids, the folded hands, the tearful eyes of one who finds their doom too frail? Dad sent her back into the world with a heart of stone. She will cast it at some country doctor, and come down to bed like a pine tree.

COSTA: I don't remember her very well, but I remember Gustava went about, after she had been here, with her hair down her back, in braids.

GART: Gustava is safe. The little fool became a woman too soon, it sent her scuttling into the garret like a rabbit, but the second time she grew important, now she is a matron at nineteen.

COSTA: I'd hate to be a girl.

GART: (*Drying his hands along his trousers*) What would mother have said? (*He plays in silence for a moment, thinking*) The great singer arrives, tonight mother would have played her scales in a fury, and brought high C to earth, as it is, I shall play the "Spring Song" as if it were entirely probable.

COSTA: What is she, a soprano?

GART: Who, Von Bartmann?

COSTA: Uh ha.

GART: Of course. High C is above any possible human emotion, the audience adores her! (*Seriously*) She is a very great artist. Her Thaïs makes women afraid of themselves, and men apologetic. That is art.

COSTA: She is handsome?

GART: Very.

COSTA: Gustava copies her too. Piled her hair up on top of her head.

GART: She will return to her bang, it's absolutely her.

COSTA: Is Von Bartmann married?

GART: You never know.

COSTA: Virgin?

GART: You can't be and sing like that, something breaks, and nature sweeps over you like an avalanche and you are married from all four corners of the earth before you know it. That's the way it is, father says.

COSTA: Isn't Dad great!

GART: Splendid! Marvelous! Liszt should have known him. Can't you see them walking out together! Liszt with that touching wart, sitting beside Dad while he plays, the beak nose rigid over counterpoint. He is strong where Liszt was weak. Liszt had grey hair, Dad's is red. Liszt had a short body, Dad's is short too, their hands are twin and their souls do not deviate. One loved the lilies of the field, the other the ways of the beast. Wouldn't Dad have looked splendid with Bismarck? They would have planned cruelties together; Dad would have plundered, Bismarck intrigued. Dad was lustful, Bismarck fecund. Bismarck a thinker, Dad a doer. Bismarck the strategist, Dad the simple; one was a peasant and a woman, the other a woman and a Jesuit. The one was powerful, the other natural. One is dead, the other is living. We shall see things.

COSTA: Dad is restless again.

GART: It's the autumn, it's Dad's time for his yearly justice. Von Bartmann is a great woman, we shall have drama.

COSTA: When does she arrive?

GART: At sun-down. The great always arrive at nightfall. Animals delight in the sun, women in the dark. Put some more wood on the fire.

COSTA: *(Moving lazily to obey)* And he will send me out to chop logs. (*He grins*)

GART: What else should you be doing?

COSTA: Nothing.

GART: Then everything is as it should be.

COSTA: Do you remember the day the authorities came and tried to make Dad send us to school?

GART: *(Gaily)* Do I remember Dad going to the school! A little red roof, seven benches, a teachers platform, a blackboard smeared with chalk and spit, pictures of Longfellow and of the local alderman, and Dad sitting back on his spine asking the principal if he understood the elements of man. "Do you know," he asked, "what makes a man desperate and what makes him happy?" And the principal, turning his eyes aloft, answered, standing on the ball of the foot, "Religion makes him happy, my dear friend, and ignorance makes him desperate."

"Wait!" snapped Man Born. "Religion makes him a coward, and education, as you understand it, makes him a monologuist in the presence of his God, instead of a disciple."

How pale the representative got, and how my father enjoyed himself. "Do you realize," says the principal, "that you are bringing your children up like heathen?" "Do you realize," quoth Dad, "that your heathen put your Europe into that bed which is now your history?"

COSTA: Well, we never went to school.

GART: "They will grow up," said the principal, "deflowering women, defaming God!" "They will grow up," continued the old man, "neither with buck-shot in the one man's part, nor with hymns in the other, but weighed evenly with the goods of their mortality, casting their shot one throw ahead, like man since the beginning of the seed.

We have but that one throw, man, before we put our face to the earth," says he. "Don't come trampling on the road and trying to make scrub-oak of my sons' trees."

GUSTAVA: *(Running excitedly into the room)* They're coming, they're coming. I heard the horses' hoofs half a mile away. I have been standing out there in the turn of the road, and now they are in sight, Dad sitting up front, and she in back.

GUSTAVA *is a girl of nineteen, dressed in a checked ging-ham gown, and with high leather boots like the boys. She is high busted, rather mature and has a pink and white, complexion, an aquiline nose like a Roman Emperor, her head crowned with a mass of coarse, pretty straw-colored hair.*

COSTA: *(Getting up)* Let's get out.
GART: *(Playing on)* No, let her enter to the dying strains of the "Unfinished Sonata."

They hear the outer door open and shut, someone shout-ing to the horses, a woman's high and pleasant voice in the entry. They all fly up the steps to the bedrooms, GUS-TAVA *leaning a moment over the banister.*

Enter MME. JULIE VON BARTMANN, *a tall, hand-some woman of thirty-eight, dressed in a long trailing gown of saffron, over which is a chinchilla wrap reach-ing to her feet. She wears a toque, and thin suede gloves are about to be removed. She looks back at* BASIL BORN, *a man of fifty, dressed in a sheepskin coat, and with a leather cap drawn well forward over thick curling hair. His legs are encased in felt boots, and dog-skin gloves dangle from his pockets. He is carrying a hat-box and a rug.*

JULIE: *(Looking slowly about)* Immense!

Thinks of removing her coat, decides to keep it on for the moment, as there is no possible place for anything unless on the chairs or tables. Pulls both gloves off, and stares around the walls, stopping at the organ. BASIL *has removed his cap, leaving the baggage near the door, he stands before the fire, warming himself.*

JULIE: Do you play?
BASIL: I did, but I had a son, and he takes my place.
JULIE: How nice. Does he play well?
BASIL: Someday he will be a great musician, he has pas-
    sion, manner—
JULIE: *(Playfully)* Haven't you?
BASIL: I have passion, but my manner has been inter-
    rupted by versatility and preoccupation.
JULIE: *(Seating herself)* Preoccupation with what?
BASIL: Instruments, madame, I play the French horn, the

cello, I compose—

JULIE: Really, and then what happens?

BASIL: Physically I am not very strong, I become tired, I lie down, thinking of history.

JULIE: Whose?

BASIL: They are before you madame.

JULIE: *(Wickedly)* Ah yes, Leda, Beatrice, after the unpardonable proximity, Venus—

BASIL: No, Liszt, Beethoven, Chopin—

JULIE: Ah yes, Chopin, he helps doesn't he?

BASIL: *(Fumbling with an oil lamp, trying to light it)* At fifty, one becomes thankful.

JULIE: *(Abruptly)* Do you farm?

BASIL: The boys a little, I have two sons, a daughter, she takes care of the pigeons, the garden—

JULIE: Where are they?

BASIL: Not far, they will be in soon.

JULIE: How old is your daughter?

BASIL: Gustava is nineteen.

JULIE: *(Calmly)* What will she think of me?

BASIL: What most pleases her.

JULIE: I am not married, that is—not married. I have not money worries. I love—peculiarity, perhaps you would call it vice. *(She raises her eyes, watching him)* Nothing astonishes me. In the night when it rains, when the lightning flashes and the thunder rolls, I do not draw my toes up, I sleep, and leave terror and superstition to the people.

BASIL: At a pinch madame, I can be a little peculiar myself.

JULIE: It begins to be something of which I am aware. I have heard that you are savage. Is it so?

BASIL: Not at all. I have a certain influence with my family, but the state does not like me.

JULIE: *(Interested)* Why not?

BASIL: You see before you a little man—

JULIE: Well?

BASIL: I am five feet seven inches. My hair curls, my mouth is firm. Peoples in places of dictatorship do not like it.

JULIE: Why?

BASIL: It reminds them that there are some things that cannot be used. I do not let my children attend school. I teach them what they know. The board of education provides dates and the speeches of officials, officers, generals, statesmen. They feel that they have done their duty if a child can render *Hamlet* backwards. So I keep my children at home, letting them do as they please—with reservations.

JULIE: Doesn't it make them nervous?

BASIL: My dear madame, I kill my own beef, pickle it, smoke it. At first my daughter Gustava (she is a gentle girl) was over fond of the sight of blood, she used to toss in her sleep, but now she has calmed down, her ankles and her wrists are thickening, her hair is abundant and blond. My daughter is simple and great, like a Greek horror, her large pale head, with its wide-set, uncalculating eyes, is like those of children who have been begotten in a massacre, and nursed on the guillotine. She can live gently from now on.

JULIE: *(Leaning a little forward)* And what are the boys like?

BASIL: Splendid! Simply splendid! Costa, the youngest, is morose. I can't say how he will be useful to nature, but he will be useful. If he had been "educated," if he had lived in a flourishing city, if he had become a dandy and worn a fashionable little moustache, he would have committed some common crime, suffered grossly and been redeemed by some monstrous and ludicrous religion. As it is, he knows just enough of beauty and of horror to know that he understands nothing. It will take him, as it will take all my children, his entire life to unravel the web of his upbringing.

JULIE: And your other son?

BASIL: Gart. Splendid too, but another type. Thin, haggard, ridden by the Ninth Symphony. He plays Beethoven as if he were going to war, and Schubert as if he were going to bed. Because he is slightly like myself, because his voice is unsettled, he is shy. He is a hard worker and does not complain that I have a weak stomach. He is very watchful of his sister. If dressed in a frock coat and set out upon a concert stage, he would resemble one of those priests who have found God too cheerful, and every woman in the audience would change her position, at least once.

JULIE: And their mother?

BASIL: Their mother is dead, but she was well chosen. In my life I have known many women, but only one who had a voice adequate for the scream of agony. That one was their mother.

JULIE: Was she beautiful?

BASIL: No madame, beautiful women do not make good martyrs. I got her from a burlesque house in the Haymarket, she played the part of a drummer, she was young then, and had a long melancholy face, like the faces of kings who have not ruled. I could see in the way she lifted her legs that she wanted to settle down, to become gross, to be a mother, to drink strong coffee, to sleep in the daytime, and at night to pour over the destiny of the Corsican. She was very simple, very lewd, she laughed at one time and not at another, she was strong but not healthy, she was pure

but much handled; she had dignity but she was pow-
erless. That madame, was the mother of my children.

JULIE: *(Simply)* And what will become of your daughter?

BASIL: She will follow her mother. She is both buxom
and coarse, I mean that in the best sense. She will become stout, it will save her from the pale existence of
those women who, from the cradle to the grave, have
but two odors: celibacy and monogamy. My daughter will be frank, neither promiscuous nor childless,
these things are for flat-chested women whose hearts
beat sideways for lack of room. She will eat, func-
tion, die, looking neither backward nor forward.

JULIE: Yet—what will she do with that ecstatic moment
when she lies, for the first time, with her lover?

BASIL: The simple, madame, put no claims on ecstasy.

JULIE: And now—what are you like?

BASIL: I am that spot on which the dead have lain, where
the grass is pale, where insects busy themselves. It
has the look of corruption, but it is the most fertile
spot in the field.

JULIE: *(Going on with the drama of exposition)* Why do
all men desire me?

BASIL: Because you come to destroy. We shall outlast
you.

JULIE: The boys?

BASIL: They also.

JULIE: *(Stroking her gloves)* Gustava?

BASIL: Particularly Gustava.

JULIE: It's a little vulgar, isn't it?

BASIL: What?

JULIE: Immunity.

BASIL: Very, but we have planned immunity from the cradle.

JULIE: Yet you do not look strong.

BASIL: Physically, no. Mentally yes. We cherish neither God, king nor courtesan.

JULIE: Why?

BASIL: Respect. If you cherish God, he becomes a fad, if you cherish kings they become despots, and if you cherish a courtesan she becomes an idiot.

JULIE: Why do you say that?

BASIL: Because she is tender, corrupt, fertile.

JULIE: You are a good father?

BASIL: Excellent. When the weather is cold I tell them everything; women, I say, are monstrous, beautiful, man is active. I say freedom exists in keeping the wood cut, the fire lit, the animals productive. Knowledge exists in knowing that the horse founders, the ship sinks, and that women, with some unknown dexterity, take comfort from anything that has no evidence.

JULIE: And when it's hot?

BASIL: They wrestle.

JULIE: And so you have reached safety, no matter how I should pitch my voice, you would be on another level.

BASIL: All nonsense aside, do you forget that I am a man?

JULIE: All nonsense aside, are you?

BASIL: Madame, what do you expect of me and my children?

JULIE: I expect, monsieur, surprise from you and your children.

BASIL: Madame, what do you sing?

JULIE: I sing love songs, Basil Born.

BASIL: But how do you sing them?

JULIE: *(Mischievously)* As if they were hymns, between the approach and the retreat of sex.

BASIL: *(Calmly)* The idiot's voice.

JULIE: No, that is sexless from default, mine from cunning. On the other hand let me at a hymn—

BASIL: Then?

JULIE: Then I have no mercy.

BASIL: *(Thrusting his head forward)* Well?

JULIE: I am willing you should play a little. *(She walks toward the door as* GUSTAVA *appears with a night-light)* But—I am noted for my detours!

BASIL: *(To his daughter)* Show that splendor to bed!

GUSTAVA *takes up the hatbox and rug.*

Curtain.

Act First

The best bedroom in the BORN *Farmhouse. Late at night.*

The room is almost in darkness. JULIE VON BARTMANN *is lying asleep. The bed is back right, a window at the head, a door, leading to the dining room at the foot. A bureau with mirror and water pitcher and bowl against the left wall. The bed is large, four posted and hung with gloomy red curtains in a rose pattern, they are drawn well back,* JULIE *is sleeping on her arm, her black hair all over the pillow, her little satin-embroidered slippers arranged neatly under the edge of the bed, a marvelous creation in silk, a peignoir of extreme French origin, lies over the back of a chair, her boxes are scattered here and there, plumes and lace and shoes.*

    GUSTAVA, *in a long night robe, a candle in her hand, opens the door softly and comes in. She stands a moment, not daring to move, puts a foot into the room definitely and quickly, never taking her eyes from the figure of the sleeping* JULIE. *She tip-toes up to the bed, putting the candle down on the dresser, and stands so, looking at her, her hands hanging at her sides.* JULIE *turns, moves, opens her eyes.*

JULIE: What is it?

GUSTAVA: It is nothing.

JULIE: *(Waking up)* Nothing? Isn't it very late?

GUSTAVA: It is two o'clock.

JULIE: *(Smiling)* Don't you sleep?

GUSTAVA: I couldn't, I lay staring up in the darkness—

JULIE: I have travelled a long way, I am very tired.

GUSTAVA: I know. I must talk to you. *(She seats herself on the edge of the bed)*

JULIE: Aren't you cold?

GUSTAVA: No, no, I am not cold.

JULIE: Now what is it you want to say to me?

GUSTAVA: I want you to make me realize what my father is. I want you to tell me about greatness.

JULIE: Well, that's difficult.

GUSTAVA: I know, but you must do it, I've read about you, how great your Thaïs is, what a note is when you sing it, everything, but I want to know more than that. I want to look at you and know everything—

JULIE: Well, what do you want to know first?

GUSTAVA: *(Holding her hands tightly)* I know one great

figure, Basil Born, but perhaps he is not a figure, I want to measure him by you.

JULIE: *(Laughing outright)* You do!

GUSTAVA: *(Gently)* Wait, don't laugh. It is like this: You were born. You were laid in a bassinet, you did not cry. You learned to walk before other children, you watched everything, and then one day, when you were three or four, you realized that you were terrible, a child of destiny. You moved along the floor, small, insignificant and tragic, because you knew that when your heart was on a level with the top of the bureau, you would suffer. You threw yourself on the floor, on your face, and kept still, terribly still, but you grew older. You did your hair around your head, you rode on a train, you were not what you used to be. And then one day a man took your fancy, you walked together under the trees, you went to small towns together, you took a boat, you were in foreign parts, you became sleepy, you went to a hotel, and he did not dare to defile you until you had shut the door, there was a great clock under a glass, and it did not go, there were a lot of vulgar red cushions and gilt chairs, and you said: "Aren't the French funny people, they may have so many dead clocks."

JULIE: Where did you get all this?

GUSTAVA: I have travelled, mother travelled, she travelled to keep herself from thinking, father was everything, but that's different. Then when that was over you forgot and you were a woman, and you were terrible again, as you were at four, and you talked to yourself. You were dressed in a tight gown without sleeves, and you kept saying to yourself, madly you kept saying it, without moving, without touching your hands: "Don't hurry me, I'll understand soon, I'll make myself understand it before it is too much for me, if only you'll give me time, if only you won't torment me, if you won't watch me, if only you will lose sight of me for an hour, one small hour—ten minutes—"

JULIE: A little girl like you, such a little country girl—

GUSTAVA: *(Unheeding)* After that you cried in your sleep, and drew yourself together.

JULIE: No, no, that's not it at all, I used to lie on my stomach, because it was such fun, and then I grew up—

GUSTAVA: Let me put my head on your arm, your perfume is so strong, and so sweet—

JULIE: *(Making room for her)* Come, put your head down, and be quiet, you funny little girl.

GUSTAVA: *(Her head on* JULIE *'s arm, quietly)* I love you.

JULIE: You too?

GUSTAVA: I love you, it is like that.

JULIE: Well, let it be like that—it is all right.

GUSTAVA: If father put up an opera house here, would you come and sing in it?

JULIE: *(Sleepily)* To the ducks?

GUSTAVA: No, no in the open fields—

JULIE: "A rowley, powley, gammon and spinach," for your brothers—

GUSTAVA: No, Thaïs. It would be like this: One night out of your great life, you would come here to sing, here, to the simple people, with their life all about them. You would be dressed in furs, yes, your face would be warmed by a very gentle fur, mole perhaps, they are beautiful, on women. We would have a towering fire, and all the lights would be lit and all of us would be quiet. And later you would drive in our sleigh, with two horses, right up to the door of the Opera House. You would hear the orchestra out there, and the lights would be over everything. And then you would come out, all powdered and jeweled, and breathing, and the people would shout and clap and raise their welcome to the high, immense and impending roof. And outside I would be waiting for you, in the snow, with my arms full of flowers, and we would drive home, and I would not speak.

JULIE: You are a clear and passionate thing, Gustava.

GUSTAVA: You will go away and I shall go on developing, until I am nothing, just myself.

JULIE: Perhaps.

GUSTAVA: Shall you love father?

JULIE: What a question.

GUSTAVA: You'd better go away then.

JULIE: Why?

GUSTAVA: He is like a woman, he is sickly but merciless. He sits long hours by the fire, then he hurries out, gives something away, a horse, a dog, and returns saying that man is unjust, you see how it is.

JULIE: Well, I will give you something. I've got a papier-mâché doll, yes, I'll give it to you.

GUSTAVA: How did you get it?

JULIE: One night, in Monte-Carlo, I cried for it, like a baby, and a man in a striped vest gave it to me, and in the morning—I kept the doll.

GUSTAVA: That's life too.

JULIE: *(Sleepily)* I used to sing my arpeggios in the morning, but my window overlooked a racing paddock, and I had to change to rooms over an inner court, where my voice could rise up undisturbed, I had to learn to sing all over again, because of the horses, their rhythm. Every day a little man, without a soul, came, in a red jockey cap and coat, to ride the most beautiful horse, looking proudly up, at the birds in the sky, as if the horse's superb body were his, then

I was angry, and I went away.

GUSTAVA: And then?

JULIE: Then I sang an aria and forgot.

GUSTAVA: Yes.

JULIE: I used to cry when I didn't get what I wanted, right away, and I pretended to everyone that it was just a fancy, and that I had not cried at all, and they were perfectly furious. I had a little uneventful lover, with a fashionable moustache, and he slapped me once, when I had done that, and I went right up to him, and I said: "Don't you understand that no one could love you, that as you are, you are utterly ridiculous? See, you have advanced in the world only so far as a little beard, and you cry—that's forgery, and I can't bear forgery, understand? It embarrasses me, and I won't be embarrassed." He simply stared at me and managed to say "extraordinary," as if someone had been dancing. And I—"Idiot!"

GUSTAVA: You said that, just that?

JULIE: Absolutely, just that.

GUSTAVA: *(Rising in bed slowly, with a living passion, though very still)* Always like that? Always?

JULIE: *(Amused)* Invariably.

GUSTAVA: You did not plan, there was no introspection. You caused no whirlwind, no man died for you. No girl, thinking of you, lay in the arms of some student thinking of you. The days came and went, there was no miracle, no dawn, no disillusion, no splendor, no horror, no irreparable harm. Nothing! Nothing! Nothing!

JULIE: *(Cruelly)* Nothing.

GUSTAVA: You did not look up, there were no dark, cumbersome gardens, the hedges were not asters, the earth was not gloomy. You did not regret and you had no forebodings. You were not incalculable, you knew no remorse, you did not rise in the night to speak to anyone saying, "I am burdened and sorrowful and bewildered?" There were no betrayals and no vengeance, no sighs, no tears, no happiness and no fear. There was neither pursuer nor pursuing. No crime and no atonement, no perversity, no struggle, no torment. The heart did not beat, the sky was not overcast, nor ominous nor lofty, the soul did not tremble, there was neither suspense nor relief, neither pleasure nor pain. Nothing! Nothing! Nothing! Deny it, deny it!

JULIE: *(Slowly)* NO—

GUSTAVA: There was no drama, you did not squander, you did not lavish, you cherished nothing, and were not cherished. You were not scorned and you did not scorn. You were careful, you counted your days, you connived at existence, you flourished tightly, you had no flights of brutality, no miscarriages of anger, no abortions of faith. You were not proud, nor high, nor terrible. Nothing! Nothing! Nothing!

JULIE: My little girl, everything was very quiet, simple, gentle.

GUSTAVA: *(Now almost hysterical)* You were never mad, nor sane, nor great! You did not kill, you knew no tempests, you were still, quiet, simple, nothing! Nothing!

JULIE: No, no, do not excite yourself, see, you are trembling, is this a child's rage, is this a child's chagrin? Come, this will not do. I was not that, but I was something else.

GUSTAVA: There is nothing else! I have named everything—let me think, don't hurry me, let me think. *(Without a pause)* No, everything was there, everything that has been, or could be, or will ever be, I've forgotten nothing, nothing, nothing!

JULIE: Yes, you have forgotten me.

GUSTAVA: *(Brought to a pause for the first time)* Shall I trust you? Why must I trust you?

JULIE: Wait a little, you shall see, you shall understand, later, later.

GUSTAVA: I could have loved you without regret or shame, that night when you might have sung, and I would have died then and been buried happily, and people could have come and looked at me, quite as they pleased, just in their usual way, looked at me and have found no sin. Not to have one remorse, nor one regret, because you would have been mine, and have gone before the hour for either.

JULIE: *(Seriously)* Look at me, here is the face of an unknown woman, there may be drama child, wait.

GUSTAVA: *(Hesitatingly)* Can you plan?

JULIE: I transpire.

GUSTAVA: *(Coming close up to her)* Can you handle children, do you know us?

JULIE: I have never reckoned with children.

GUSTAVA: Now you have come to it, we are here, what are you going to do?

JULIE: Wait, you must go away now—you must sleep.

GUSTAVA: Good night. *(She exits)*

Curtain.

Act Second

SCENE FIRST

Time: early morning of the next day.

GUSTAVA is seated at the table, cutting out pictures from the magazine, sections of the Sunday newspapers, pasting them together. COSTA enters, throws a bridle and saddle into the corner.

COSTA: What are you doing?

GUSTAVA: Pictures.

COSTA: What for?

GUSTAVA: For Julie, they might please her. I've put the general in back of the lady at the opera, they are listening to "Pagliacci"—But they are thinking of the corruption of human nature.

COSTA: *(Coming up to look)* The general has the look, sloping shoulders, thick hips, pinched nostrils. *(Grinning)* And where is Julie von Bartmann at this moment?

GUSTAVA: She lies in bed, she stretches her arms, she looks out into the orchard, she, she thinks of getting up, but it is difficult, she must bathe her face in cold water, then there are lotions and creams and powders, rouge, perfume, kohl, that's for the eyes. She polishes her nails, with quick short strokes, she must choose a gown, slippers to match, she must think of rings, earrings, bracelets. Finally she comes down, radiant, rested, dramatic.

COSTA: Wrong. She left the house a good hour or more ago, dressed for hunting, carrying a rifle, Dad following her.

GUSTAVA: *(Surprised)* Which way did they go?

COSTA: Into the back woods, not much to hunt, but she simply couldn't wait, you could see it in her shoulders—

GUSTAVA: Can she shoot?

COSTA: How do I know? You hear shots, both firing at the same moment like a duel, but all they will bring home after all, is one little frightened rabbit between them.

GUSTAVA: I hadn't thought of her somehow, as a hunter. *(Absently)* What do you think of her?

COSTA: I don't know, what do you think of her?

GUSTAVA: Beautiful.

COSTA: Uh huh.

GUSTAVA: Don't you think she is beautiful?

COSTA: Yes.

GUSTAVA: Where's Gart?

COSTA: Feeding the pigeons. Wait until Julie sees that.

GUSTAVA: Why wait until she sees that?

COSTA: He is shy—

GUSTAVA: Shy? *(Pushing her pictures aside, leaning on her elbows)* Isn't it a funny thing, first we are alone, months, nothing happens, the farmers go by on the road to church, their children up on their knees, they spit into the dust, they talk of the harvest, and we sit here, thinking, eating, keeping up the fire, then, like a clap of thunder comes Mme. Von Bartmann, soprano, in a yellow dress, saying "Immense, Immense!"

COSTA: And dad walking around and around the house.

GUSTAVA: *(Walking about)* I know, you don't like any of this, like an animal that has smelled blood, it hurts your heart. There's a man's business in the world— somewhere, *(Turning suddenly about)* and I'm here, a little stout perhaps, yet I shall not be as father says, he has made a mistake, he has overlooked something.

COSTA: *(Amused)* Has he?

GUSTAVA: He hasn't overlooked me, but he has over-looked what I shall do with me—that's another thing—

COSTA: Oh well—

GUSTAVA: No, you can be quiet forever, if you like, but I'm only quiet—so far—
COSTA: What are you going to do?
GUSTAVA: I am going to become unbelievable just at that moment when my father says: "Behold, my daughter!"

At this moment JULIE, *followed by* BASIL, *enters, she is dressed in a smart hunting costume and she carries a gun,* BASIL *carries a hunting bag but slightly distended.*

BASIL: My son Costa.
COSTA: *(Awkwardly)* Pleased—
JULIE: *(Smiling)* Charming! Charming!
BASIL: We have shot a hare, we do not know whose hare it is, we both shot at once, and it lay over still, on its side, quite dead.
COSTA: I said so.
JULIE: I haven't shot since I was seventeen, a bad shot, but vicious.
BASIL: *(Giving the bag to* GUSTAVA*)* Take it my dear.

GUSTAVA *takes it and passes* GART *coming in as she goes out.* BASIL *opens his mouth to introduce his son* GART, *but is stopped.*

GART: Mme. Von Bartmann.

JULIE: Gart, I believe.

GART: Gart.

JULIE: Your father tells me you wrestle.

GART: We do.

JULIE: And that you play—superbly.

GART: Often.

JULIE: You must play for me.

BASIL: He will play for you, but now we must trot the horses. *(He picks up the bridle, motions* COSTA *to pick up the saddle, and goes toward the door)*

JULIE: But you mustn't all go, leave me one son.

COSTA *goes out.*

BASIL: He plays, you sing, we shall hear you out in the yard as we take the turn. *(He exits)*

JULIE: Well?

GART: Well?

JULIE: Perhaps it was you, after all, that I wanted to be alone with, simply you.

GART: Why?

JULIE: Because I do not like interrupting my existence, for instance I could tell you what I was like at eighteen, you simply would not listen, no, you would hear me, but you would not make it live, you would respect it like a dead fire, but Gustava—she would look at me with bright unwavering eyes and say, "When you were a child, when you were only four, then you realized that you were terrible." One must be gentle with women like that, they so easily become "figures." You wouldn't want to know me, really know me before I talked with you, would you?

GART: No.

JULIE: See, that's immense, let us begin then when I was twenty.

GART: No, eighteen.

JULIE: Why did you say that?

GART: *(Slowly)* Because I am twenty.

JULIE: Yes, but my twenty wasn't the least like your twenty, not a bit of it, well, will you believe it, I was very sentimental, oh to the point of tears, to the edge of melancholy. I have never outgrown the sadness and the tenderness evoked by gazing, in my early youth, upon Rembrandt's "Girl with a Dove," of the "Moor" framed in wooden oak leaves, wherein a white girl, abounding in pale hair, dressed in shift of muslin, girdled with a satin rope, leans back upon the shoulder of the moor, dark, bearded, and with woman's hands. There was something secret, something unspeakably mournful and proud in the way the beard thinned toward the cleft in the chin, ceased, exposing the bare lip, and took up its strength slowly again until it reached the cheekbone, dark and certain....

Then there were faded yellow satin slippers in a leather trunk, beaded, small, unwalking, my mother's; the printed white silk of her wedding gown, stained with the spilt milk of the first too voluptuous breast, smelling of lavender, folded lace on silk. The picture of my father, he was a student then, an Englishman, he had the air of Oxford, the long soft chin, the thin light imperial, the fine hair of those who perish early, the nose of a hangman, the eyes of a sailor, and the mouth that looked, in that face, as if it would be the first to know the tender and terrible approach of dissolution. And in his hand he held a hat, with a long nap that I had never stroked. Do you understand all this?

GART: Yes, I know.

JULIE: *(Brightly, quickly, not looking at him)* I loved the past, I adored the dead, I was a connoisseur of tombs, but that Costa would understand better than you.

GART: Why would he understand that better than I?

JULIE: Because Costa is a brute, a beast, a beast understands, without thought, all the ageless sorrows of simple functions, life, death. Costa could love and kill, but he would be outwitted, because no man dies twice, but let that go, you will not understand that, you will be angry, and anger is not right now, not for this—I succumbed to the bead wreaths, the porcelain flowers under their glass bosses, the photographs so poignantly outdone by time. The straight, stiff tin leaves, the embroiders, lambrequins, the spiral candles, the Virgin made personal, and occupied, the perishable suffering of the bereaved cut in imperishable stone by preoccupied lapicides. That isolated enclosure of the fantasies of sorrow, couched in silence, like an empty birdcage, wherein the twittering of the mourners rises, amazed and disconcerted.

This was in France. Then I began to sing, by way of the dead and by way of cigarette prizes. That surprises you, let me explain. With every package of cigarettes my father smoked, came a pin button with the glazed photograph of some dead but historic actress upon it. Rejane, Coquelin, one of Lotta Crabtree, sometimes the living, Lilly Langtree, Bernhardt, well, he gave them to me, and I kept them under my pillow. The white tide of full breasts, the profound legs, the huge sleeves, the peaceful lace, the hair low on the neck and forehead, the rising ruff, the clasped hands, the paste jewels, the beaded buskins, the sequined gowns, the plush, the velvet, the brocade, rucked, twisted, mauled in an emotional crisis of another century, small feet, plump insteps, glittering hips, linen roses, gauntlets, rapiers crowns. My heart beat, I took my hair down, I put a cherry between my teeth, drew my lips back, moved toward the mirror. It was a small mirror, I leaned it on a chair, I pinned my skirt up, and realized that another tradition would begin where my legs started. Why? Because they were so dreadfully thin, like a boy's, with a little diamond-shaped kneecap. I lifted the mirror to the cushions. I looked at my breasts, I adored them, I promised them that one day, when they were less independent, I would lace them tightly, and wear violets for them. Then I hung the mirror up, and looked once more into a face. A small chin, a long nose, a mouth too large, eyes not focused, the eyes you see on women who stake their lives on more than one destination. I tried out passion, hate, grief, love, laughter. The laughter was an idiot's, the grief was a child's, but the passion was satisfactory. I was afraid, I locked the door. I had been guilty of untimeliness. Then, I was twenty one.

GART: And after that?

JULIE: After that I discovered the secret of "personality"—do everything a moment before you can bear it.

GART: Do what?

JULIE: I noticed everything, for instance, I noticed all the vulgar things one must do to go on living.

GART: Yes.

JULIE: I began to look at my father when he was preoccupied, when he eased himself from one position to another; at my mother when she laughed, throwing her head back. I looked at everything, upside-down, just as it was, noticed how large her nostrils were, the roof of her mouth, at the under part of the chin, at the white of her eyes. I watched my brother when he thought he was unobserved. I did everything disgusting I could think of, just because I did not want to, nothing, positively nothing escaped me, I used to see humor in the shapes sewn into trousers that the body might sit.

GART: What have I to do with all this?

JULIE: Why nothing, that's why I'm telling it to you. Now let us come to my mother. She was a German and Italian, but she became, to outward appearances, an incurable Englishwoman before she had lived in England five years. She had the Englishwoman's passion for derbies, she had long teeth and she wore tweed. She used to go alone to the "chimes," sitting well forward, leaning well back. She carried a cane, and she experienced the most extraordinary emotions. She had not read much, she had not seen many people, yet when her time came, she drank cocktails with Mme. Wilde, went to Oscar's teas, and wondered, under the subdued lights, why Mme. Wilde looked so monstrous in dotted swiss. She had seen rape committed in Holland Park, and she had heard a man preach in Shepherd Bush. "Try to believe in eternity," she said, "because it may keep you from doing transient injustice during your time." Nevertheless she was incensed when my father brought home a flute and tried to play it with the technique of a trombonist. "Each instrument has its stops," she said. She used to stalk through London admiring the Royal Guards, because in some small way their magnificent build was a protection to the throne, and she would say, "There isn't a spine in the Bartmann family that has forgotten to sit as if it were on a throne no matter what it was sitting on." And she emphasized the "what" when we were very young, and learning.

GART: Then you took your mother's name?

JULIE: Heavens yes, how could a woman sing under the name of Petersford?

GART: I like your mother.

JULIE: I liked my mother. She was matchless for her continuations. How she would always scent the debacle before it occurred. "If you go out with this man," she would remark, "you will be sorry for it," and I was. "If you believe a word of his speeches, you are a fool, they are lies," and they were. "And if," she would add, "you are inclined to become emotional when So-and-So plays this afternoon at the concert, remember that he is falsifying Brahms and thinking of Wagner," or "That fellow cannot play Tristan—in three bars, Isolde will be a fallen woman."

GART: I do not understand.

JULIE: Never mind. And she often remarked, "Don't imagine that you are misunderstood, for the probability is, you are not."

GART: Your father never said anything?

JULIE: Heavens, like a magpie, here and there and incessantly, but he said pretty much-what he meant, and it was often very dull, yet once my mother had a thrilling scene when I was thirty. "That child," he said, "is none of mine," and my mother answered, crying right out, "She was, William, while I was carrying her, but she soon lost the scent."

GART: And now you are older.

JULIE: Much older.

GART: And now you play with us.

JULIE: And now I play with you. At this knee boys have trembled, and girls become hysterical, because I sing for the people. Do you know what it is to sing for the people, what it means to sing for the people? It means that I know where they fall, and I commence my song from that, a voice that springs straight up from an uncensored knowledge, giving them the feeling that there is a majestic spectacle going on to an end unseen by the eye of man. But do you think I was glad that I triumphed? I was sorry, I was stricken, I was ashamed. I was the magnificent flourish to their meanness, profiteer of their shortcomings, my voice overshot the mark, as Christ overshot the mark, and instead of despising me for it, instead of seeing that the spring and the font of that flourish was in their very limitations, that it caught its balance there and there learned its tricks, they adored me, they let me play with their inadequacy, they let me wanton with the raveled edges of their souls. I had gone out to be happy, and I had found the terrible excitement of the thief—I was a grim girl and a humorous woman. I was sinless but defiled, as the saints are who are prayed to by no clean hand. I was truthful, but I had the lies of the world packed beneath my heart. I was thoughtful, but reckless. How? Because I had known the names for everything, but not the taste. I became pitiless because I had forgiven everything and everyone, before it was required of me, I smelled their dead before they had murdered them.

GART: *(Rising up)* Yet I am preoccupied. My father lives here from day to day. He goes to bed and I see him sitting there as if he wanted to be told that he is a great man, yet I cannot speak to him, because he wants to

be great and yet unobserved, he is frightened, his face
says, "Forget me, I am great." And in the morning he
says, "Play me something," and I play.

JULIE: And now he obsesses you.

GART: I love him because I am afraid to have known
him so well, because he has hidden nothing from me,
I have become abject.

JULIE: And you might have loved me.

COSTA *enters, goes up to* GART, *strikes him on the cheek.*

COSTA: *(Softly)* You!

GART: *(Locking with him, overturning tables and chairs
in their struggle)* You!

JULIE: It has begun!

Curtain.

Act Second

SCENE SECOND

Early the following morning, about sunrise.

BASIL BORN'S *bedroom. He sleeps in one of two beds almost in the centre of a small room with a sloping roof. Door back left.* GART *occupies the other bed.* BASIL *sleeps heavily,* GART *is awake. He rises on his elbow, and looks at his father. He lies back, there is silence for a minute, rising again he stretches out his arms, touching his father's hair.*

BASIL *moves, turns upon his back.*

GART: *(Softly)* Did I wake you Dad?

BASIL: Yes, yes, what is it? Do you want to come in with me?

GART: Yes. *(He gets up out of his own bed and lies down beside his father)*

BASIL: *(Sleepily putting his arms over him, pulling the bed covers up about his shoulders)* Go to sleep.

GART: No, I've been thinking. *(He speaks in such a strange manner that his father raises his head)*

BART: Thinking?

GART: Is Julie von Bartmann a good woman?

BASIL: No.

GART: Why?

BASIL: Erotic.

GART: What do you mean?

BASIL: Beautiful, damaged, therefore more beautiful.

GART: How damaged?

BASIL: Later, I'm sleepy.

GART: No, we must talk now. I must know now,

BASIL: Very well, deranged—a sight-seer.

GART: What has she seen?

BASIL: Well, for instance, she knows what passion in man is.

GART: What is passion in man?

BASIL: I've explained all that.

GART: No, you have not explained. What is this passion that she knows?

BASIL: Well, suppose—But why must I talk now?

GART: I must know now, this morning, before I begin the day.

BASIL: She has seen a man tremble. "What is this?" she says. "This is yours," he answers. She comes toward him with a lively step, perhaps there are tears in her eyes, for she is submissive. "Give me something no one has ever given a woman." And he answers, "I have only that which has been given since the beginning of the world." "What is that?" she asks, and he answers, trembling still more, clasping his hands, on which the veins stand out, "Grossness." And she sees him with humid eyes approaching her, looking very divine and very ugly. "Wait!" she cries, and he begins to breathe heavily. He knocks over a chair, she has regained her equilibrium; there is always some disaster in a man's walk that gives her back her safety, if she wants it. "Animal!" she says. "Mate of that," he answers and comes down upon her.

GART: Then, then—

BASIL: Then she knows still more.

GART: Is that all?

BASIL: No, that's not even a beginning, but sleep now, it's early.

GART: No, we cannot sleep. Tell me then what does she do.

BASIL: For all drama there is an audience. Women are the audience.

GART: And then?

BASIL: Then perhaps she observes injustice. The curtain goes up on injustice, and she is in the pit, dressed for the scene. A low white gown, a corsage of lilies, a hand of brilliants, a fallen fur wrap. She settles herself in her chair, she has a feeling of expectation, warm, comforting, ecstatic. This is what she sees— one man betraying another. She does not take sides, she pities, she does not judge, she waits like a child for the *denouement*. Citizen A and B are acting out the travesty of emotions. Citizen A cries to the jury, "Behold the man, he has cheated me, he came to buy a sheep and he stole a cow." "He lies," retorts citizen B, "I ordered a cow and he sends me a sheep!" And all the while your Julie smiles behind her opera glass- es, best German make, covered with leather, sold in quantities, and does not take sides. She says within herself, "What is this divine difference between cow and sheep that makes the one a prize and the other a default? Was the cow sick and the sheep healthy," she asks, "or were both ailing, or were both of se- lect stock?" And the injustice continues. "Lock the man up," says the jury, "give the dealer six months for the lack of a cow, and the purchaser seven for the acquisition of a sheep." "What," says Julie von Bartmann to herself, "is one man's injustice valuable to the extent of six months and the other to the extent of seven, yet if so, which injustice is the more price- less?" And once again she knows more.

GART: Then—

BASIL: She simply goes from one to another, from scene to scene, until the end.

GART: What is the end?

BASIL: The scenes were the world's, but the end is hers.

GART: Why?

BASIL: Because one dies of oneself. This she has observed too.

GART: How?

BASIL: By death in others. Passion in others, injustice in others, have pointed the way. A man dies, she is spectator again. She sits beside his bed. "Open the windows," he says. She opens them. "Are you comfortable?" she inquires, still the onlooker, and he says yes he is comfortable. He begins to ramble in his mind. He recalls his youth, he too has lived through much. He begins to babble of his student days, trying to do impossible sums in algebra, but he loses the thread of this agony. He is old, he is selfish, the old are always selfish, degradingly selfish when death comes. Why? Because they have lived up all their disinterested days, and now, with the last hour, they concentrate on themselves, they concentrate on that little moment of life that is fading out like a drop of water in the sum. With a maniacal, a super-human effort, they watch themselves fade, trying to establish a renewal. They demand another pillow, they send it away, they whimper for air, and refuse it, because it is impersonal, they want light, and call to instant darkness, because it is for all mankind, and in the dark they die debased by their own dissolution. They watch themselves, unredeemed by any other corporeal body, for this they curse the living and go to death ingloriously. And all the while Julie von Bartmann tends them with sighs and dabs of a lace handkerchief, and is not troubled overmuch. She listens only for the last words, as if they were of some secret medical value, she holds them as all-important. This is an error, they are only important because they are not covered up by others.

GART: This is exactly what I wanted to know.

BASIL: And now I am entirely waked up, and I will find it difficult to sleep.

GART: Then what does Julie do?

BASIL: Julie, Julie, Julie! Is that all that possesses you?

GART: *(Simply)* Isn't that enough?

BASIL: Too much, remember everything, and don't ask yourself useless questions.

GART: Are there any useless questions?

BASIL: Hundreds, thousands, people spend their lives asking them.

GART: Who shall I ask if I do not ask you?

BASIL: Observe.

GART: Is this then all that makes Julie not a very good woman?

BASIL: Precisely.

GART: What would have made her a good woman?

BASIL: There are no good women, they see too much from the start. If you lock them in a dungeon, in solitary confinement, from the cradle to the grave, they see too much, they look into their hearts, and in their hearts there are even worse scenes than enacted by man.

GART: What scenes?

BASIL: They act the precise drama of man, only they act it before God. This is religion.

GART: And this is all?

BASIL: Not all, but it is all I can tell you.

GART: Why is this all that you can tell me?

BASIL: Because everything else is unexplainable.

GART: *(Slowly)* Then you admit it.

BASIL: I admit what?

GART: Your failure.

BASIL: What failure?

GART: Your failure to finish what you have begun.

BASIL: *(Disturbed)* And what have I begun and failed to finish?

GART: My life.

BASIL: You must finish your life.

GART: No, you must finish my life. You have begun it and you must see it through. If you had let me alone, if you had told me nothing it would have been my fault, and no one could be blamed for what happened, but you did not let me alone, therefore you must continue.

BASIL: I have tried to make you safe for tragedy, by telling you every step toward tragedy.

GART: And when tragedy is reached, what have you to say?

BASIL: When the time comes, you will find yourself prepared.

GART: The time has come, and I am not prepared.

BASIL: What do you mean? What is the matter?

GART: I have come to something that I do not understand, or only in one way, I think it would not be your way.

BASIL: What have you come to, what do you want to know?

GART: Whether I must kill myself, or you.

BASIL: *(In terror)* What is this? What is this?

GART: I must find out alone. Is it you, or is it me.

BASIL: You are sick, go to bed, you are sick!

GART: No, I am not sick. I'll stay here, until the end.

BASIL: *(Frightened, trying, another tack)* See here son, you are ill and talking like a madman, I cannot allow it, threatening your own father.

GART: Who else should I threaten?

BASIL: Come, come, go to bed.

GART: Are you afraid?

BASIL: Of you, my own son?

GART: Still you are afraid, I think, you who have always seemed to fear nothing, you who were prepared for everything in the world you to whom nothing could happen that would startle you, you who could not be taken unawares, now it appears you are taken unawares.

BASIL: Come, what is it you want?

GART: To lay open the heart, yours or mine.

BASIL: Do you realize that you are a child, but just turned twenty, that you have seen nothing, known nothing except what I have shown you, that from now on you must live your life yourself?

GART: Yes, I realize that, and that is what now you must realize. I have been told too much. Perhaps after you are gone, I can understand, everything may be clear, I will be able to go on. But if you are afraid, it is horrible, horrible!

BASIL: *(he tries to slip out of bed unnoticed)* Would you take such a chance?

GART, *with a slow but sure movement, reaches his arm*

over him.

GART: I am not afraid, I will take what comes. If one thing fails, there is still another. I will go all the way.

He makes a movement, and with a cry of terror and with superhuman strength BASIL *leaps out of bed, and darts about the room, crying in a high breaking voice.*

BASIL: I never said I understood anything, it was simply that I was not dull. Just because this is my life, why must it be tragic! Wait, this is your father's body, your father's body! (He falls against the door, turning over on his face, weeping) Shameful, shameful! It is all shameful!

Someone is heard running up the steps toward the door.

Curtain.

Act Third

SCENE FIRST

Afternoon of the same day.

BASIL *enters with* GUSTAVA.

BASIL: Where is my son?

GUSTAVA: Gart? He is in the other room.

BASIL: Is anybody about?

GUSTAVA: Julie.

BASIL: Where?

GUSTAVA: In the garden—she has been walking under the trees. A long time.

BASIL: Well, I shall stay here.

GUSTAVA: *(Nervously)* Shall you need anything?

BASIL: No, I shall need nothing.

GUSTAVA: I will close the windows.

She closes the windows and goes out. BASIL *left alone, takes up the French Horn, tries the valves, turns it over, running his hand along its length, pauses, but does not play it. He puts it down. He avoids the windows for a few moments, walks about the room, shrugs his shoulders, finds himself in front of the windows and stands there.* JULIE *passing looks up, smiles.* BASIL *does not show whether he has seen her or not—in a few moments* JULIE *can be heard in the outer hall singing a little. She comes in lightly, quickly.*

JULIE: What's the matter with everybody this morning? I have been out hours and seen nothing but the house cat.

BASIL: It's that way sometimes.

JULIE: Is it? Well it has been very much that way for hours.

BASIL: Julie—

JULIE: Basil.

BASIL: Mme. Von Bartmann.

JULIE: Monsieur Born.

BASIL: Now that's over, let us continue.

JULIE: I give you the lead.

BASIL: Madame, I want victory.

JULIE: Whose?

BASIL: I write no biography in foreign beds. My own.

JULIE: *(Leaning on the organ, smiling faintly)* What have you done with it?

BASIL: I have kept it from the world. I have not bowed down for it, I have found it in my own home, and I have held it there. You understand me, I do not have to beat about the bush. Then, you will say, it is a very small thing. And if I grant you that, what have you gained? My pride may be very small, it may be, from your worldly point of view, very tiny indeed. For you, even it may not exist, precisely so it is mine. It is not universal, it makes no such claim, is indebted to no multitude, it is lonely, and limited, but it has sufficed.

JULIE: For what?

BASIL: For my children.

JULIE: Well?

BASIL: It is threatened.

JULIE: Threatened! It is shaken, shaken! I know, I have been with your daughter. She thinks life is a profound depth within an immortal abyss. She is a biographer on a grand scale. She would include the evidence of man in her own scene. She is a historian on a vast plane. One god is not enough for her, nor one catastrophe. She would take the canvas of mankind and paint over that the image of her heart. What if I were to say to her, "All the simple beasts, soft-hosed and hard-hoofed, lie down in multitude, and rise up in multitude, waiting for their timely end. Things burrow in the earth, and pass in the clear water, and ride in the thin air; the days are and the nights are, and man is, and is not"? She would stand there, fingering that poignant little bodice, and she would say, turning on me her bright and shining eyes, "Yes?"

BASIL: Do not resort to my daughter.

JULIE: My dear man, she has taken refuge in the world; that world will resort to her.

BASIL: Madame, you fence well.

JULIE: That is my courtesy toward my opponent.

BASIL: And yet it is illegal.

JULIE: What then? Shall I capsize my heart and play the beggar, or stress some other point? Then how is this: Mme. Von Bartmann is not satisfied with the comedy, as it has been presented to her. Can she preserve her honor, her peculiar kind of honor, and still consider herself a witty woman, yet no man's baggage to carry to the very ends of perdition? What then does this Mme. Von Bartmann, caring not a fig for this or that, but relax concern with, let us say, the youngest and the beastliest of the Borns, a boy with a bull neck and a passion for rape, and there proceed to be her most contrary?

"My dear boy," she says, "if I could figure out in what way you might be best construed, that way should I take, and think nothing of it, but as you are, after all, a most model scavenger, and ever true to your high conceptions of indecency, even a prude in your unfailing baseness, all I can offer are my reverse standards." And what would Mme. Von Bartmann secure? Why so cunning a retort, that man cannot think it. Casting his arms out he cries: "Lord, Lord, why hast thou forsaken us!"

BASIL: Madame, I am an old man, and do not follow you.

JULIE: It is not sufficient? Then this. Mme. Von Bartmann takes another day, and this with that shy, gentle elder son, half musician, half human. She appears in the Stalls of the Garrick, attired in such a way that speculation lies a scant half inch below the breast bone, and nothing much above the knee, with this young ascetic, clad in the lankiest homespun, carrying a cane riddled with nails, and wearing a bowler hat. She, behind her feather fan, continues throughout the play to make him realize that she is of another turn of mind, and not a simple one either, producing in him the liveliest concern for his state, which now and again betrays itself in hoarse laughter, now in tears. "Have you no other values than these?" she cries, when by dint of excessive mapping, pinching and plaguing in all its rarest forms, no saint appears.

"None other," he answers and with a mighty resounding thwack, upon those parts she has most carefully preserved for her own comfort, lets it stand.

BASIL: Madame, permit me, in my turn, to be untimely, and remember it later, remember that I spoke out a thing that should have come later. You are a beautiful woman, you are a great woman, you are an exceedingly clever woman, I have not been indifferent— forgive me—

JULIE: That is not among my accomplishments.

BASIL: I accept your rebuke.

JULIE: Am I here, Basil, to set your fences back, restake your claim, circumscribing myself to your borders? You want victory, well, rearrange your victory, are you too old? So, that's where the enemy overtakes us; it is something you have to submit to, it is the inevitable. The inevitable is a nasty word, a cruel word, it is the person who goes on walking when you lie down to rest, it has no mercy, no tenderness and it understands no quarter. It has no heart you see, therefore no place open to attack, it knows nothing but endurance, well, and who shall say which shall endure, that is not for you or me, it is nothing that can be foreseen, it is nothing you can supplicate or pray to, and when it is beaten, if ever—

BASIL: When it is beaten—

JULIE: It is not there to praise you, it does not applaud. And there you are. It is a lonely thing and no man has thought enough of it to try for it, why should you? It offers no human reward. Why do you torment yourself?

BASIL: *(Abruptly)* I had a mother.

JULIE: Are you all she planned you should be?

BASIL: I hope—

JULIE: Ah unhappy mother, twice-damned woman, you stayed within her hopes, do you know, a woman never forgives that—

BASIL: You misunderstood me. She had no hopes, she was a splendid woman, she regarded me as she regarded the world, as a strategic possibility.

JULIE: A brave woman.

BASIL: A brave, a very brave woman, a timid woman. Small and emotional she did not stand over five feet in her slippers, she was an invalid, but she played her hand like a general; in placing her men, and I was one of them, she said: "Remember that, like the king in chess, you can move in any direction, for you there is no shot in the back, you have no back to be shot in, you cannot retreat, nor can you say you were defeated by an attack in the rear—

JULIE: Well?

BASIL: I have remembered.

JULIE: Yet you have the unmistakable signs of one who is suffering from a wound in the shoulder.

BASIL: Madame, I have not claimed to be unwounded, but I shall not fall from an unseen shot.

JULIE: I am not going to give you my understanding. As I said, there is in inevitability neither company nor approval.

BASIL: You then are, you think, inevitability—

JULIE: *(Smiling)* You think.

BASIL: Madame, I repeat, you fence well.

JULIE: That is also inevitable.

BASIL: But—

JULIE: But?

BASIL: I do not like the shape of your rapier.

JULIE: No. What you do not like is crescendo, we approach the finale, the last movement. You cannot prevent it, you did what you could, a slow courtship of a preoccupied mother. The first child is born, then the second and the third. The theme enters, it begins to return, it repeats itself swifter, swifter, louder, louder, faster, faster! and you, you are helpless. You composed a sonata, and it turns into a march, a gallop, an attack. It was to have been a garden, and it is a battlefield, it was to have been the moonlight and it is the sun, it was to have been a ballad, a chant, at worst a hosanna, and suddenly the hosanna is the great beast of the soul, lowing oblivion, trampling down your visions—a little composer done to death by a composition that blared beyond your will, *retard! dulcemelos! crescendo! fortissimo! Voila!* You are a hungry man, and have dined off your children to the bone!

BASIL: *(Now, his back to the audience, leaning his full weight on the table and bringing his face to the level of the mirror, a face distorted with anguish)* You see, there, muscular contraction—insulting to a woman of sensibilities. Leave me—

Curtain.

Act Third

SCENE SECOND

Toward evening of same day.

The drawing room. Large, with three windows looking out into the road. Books, a sofa, a wall cabinet, rugs etc. Doors in left wall and back centre right. Pegged beams, but pictureless walls. On a white marble pedestal stands a bust of Chopin. COSTA *is busy cleaning a rifle, near an open fireplace to one side of the door on left.* JULIE*'s voice can be heard in another room talking to* COSTA.

JULIE'S VOICE: Aren't you coming out?

COSTA: No.

JULIE'S VOICE: Never?

COSTA: I'm busy.

JULIE'S VOICE: Cleaning a rifle?

COSTA: Cleaning a rifle.

JULIE: *(Appearing in the doorway)* You know, in the three days I've been here I don't believe any of you have been out as far as the well.

COSTA: We have just the same.

JULIE: *(Coming in)* And you never speak to each other *en famille.*

COSTA: What do you mean?

JULIE: *(Walking over to the window, looking out)* You all seem so separate, you know, in a way—

COSTA: It wasn't that way. Not at all.

JULIE: You've changed? *(*COSTA *does not answer)* That's the third wagon that has been by today, and you don't even look. *(Still no remark)* Who is your nearest neighbor?

COSTA: A widow, she has a child.

JULIE: A daughter.

COSTA: No, a son.

JULIE: No daughter nevertheless?

COSTA: A little girl.

JULIE: Ah, twelve?

COSTA: Fourteen.

JULIE: And her name is Lily, and she has yellow hair, sticking straight up on end, and she can't spell cat.

COSTA: Her name is Fritzi Collins, and her hair hangs down, and it's black... and she can spell anything, lightning, thunder, danger—

JULIE: I see, but her mother is stupid, *(He does not answer)* very heavy, probably, reads *Pilgrim's Progress,* and had children just to help along the family album? *(No answer, she turns from the window)* Why don't you speak?

COSTA: I don't talk much?

JULIE: You can't just stand there *(Laughing)*. Don't you understand?

COSTA: Yes *(Lower)* some things.

JULIE: *(Walking about the room)* For instance?

COSTA: *(Bent over his work)* What are you?

JULIE: A woman, a woman, a woman.

COSTA: That is all you can tell me?

JULIE: Why no. Do you know anything about women?

COSTA: No.

JULIE: Nothing at all? Their shape?

COSTA: No, I don't know their shape.

JULIE: What is in their hearts?

COSTA: I don't know.

JULIE: Their heads?

COSTA: I don't know.

JULIE: What they feel?

COSTA: I don't know what they feel.

JULIE: Have you ever imagined?

COSTA: Yes.

JULIE: Have you an "ideal"?

COSTA: No.

JULIE: Why?

COSTA: They mix up, all together, I try and then—the scene changes.

JULIE: Into?

COSTA: If I think of a woman, there's always someone else with her.

JULIE: Wonderful! Go on.

COSTA: I'm not clever.

JULIE: Nevertheless

COSTA: It makes me angry.

JULIE: Of course. How do you manage?

COSTA: I don't manage.

JULIE: You fight, yet that must be, you are brutal, your father is brutal too, you know, and Gustava, only that's something else, she is brutally spiritual. Now I, for instance, am nothing of these things. I am simply—timely.

COSTA: Isn't that—brutal?

JULIE: Of course it is. But you see I am also a little exhausted.

COSTA: Well?

JULIE: Well that makes all the difference in the world, I am curious to the point of amusement, you to the point of discovery.

COSTA: Is that better?

JULIE: Worse, much worse. Someday I shan't be thinking of any of you anymore.

COSTA: And what shall I be doing?

JULIE: Wondering what has become of me.

COSTA: Are you sure?

JULIE: Positive.

COSTA: If you are wrong?

JULIE: You see, I should not mind—even that.

COSTA: *(Quietly)* Curious.

JULIE: Yes, curious.

COSTA: Yet I should like to do something.

JULIE: What with?

COSTA: My life.

JULIE: Well? *(She throws herself on the couch)*

COSTA: Like this: The sky was dark, it began to rain.

JULIE: What do you mean?

COSTA: Like that, simple. It was dark, and it began to rain. A man, a young man, is walking along the road, it is summer. He listens to the croaking of the frogs in the valley, one, two, three, then many, he does not turn his head, he breathes the air, cool from the mountains. A carriage passes him, it is the school teacher, he knows by the color and the pattern of her dress. She bounds from side to side over the heavy ruts, into puddles, through mud, thinking of early history, and is gone in an instant. The people in the town light their lamps, one, two, three like the frogs they begin, and then there are hundreds. The church bells rings, and a pack of dogs quarrels in the firelight.

JULIE: And the man?

COSTA: He does not stop. I am that man.

JULIE: But that's not making a life, that's letting it alone.

COSTA: Is it?

JULIE: That is all it is.

COSTA: Yet I am that man.

JULIE: Come here. I want to talk to you. *(COSTA approaches slowly, carrying his gun with him)* Haven't you ever been alone, quite alone with a girl?

COSTA: *(Reluctantly)* Yes.

JULIE: Quite alone?

COSTA: Yes.

JULIE: Where?

COSTA: By the pond.

JULIE: What were you doing?

COSTA: Nothing. Then suddenly we were wrestling, we wrestled by the edge and suddenly, too, she slipped and fell in, and she didn't say a word. She just lay there, looking at me. There wasn't much water, it was not deep.

JULIE: Well, wasn't she angry?

COSTA: It wasn't muddy, it was the overflow of the rain, it had rained days and days, and it overflowed between two banks, that was all.

JULIE: And you picked her up?

COSTA: No, I didn't. I just stood there, and she lay there and we looked at each other, and then she got up and went through the fence, not speaking to me.

JULIE: Went where?

COSTA: Home.

JULIE: And you did not follow her, and you were not sorry?

COSTA: I was not sorry.

JULIE: *(Smiling)* What were you? *(*COSTA *does not answer)* I know, it is simple, you could feel nothing because she had no history, this little girl was Fritzi Collins—for of course it was she—daughter of a pointless mother. It's hard to make a beginning, neither of you could do it. Here, for instance, is a history, on this you could begin: One night in Vienna, a woman, tall with splendid shoulders appears in the front box at the opera. It is toward the end of the season. She is accompanied by an officer, a very influential person, a man of great strength, a man of forty, large across the back, but thin through. He is used to women, he has always had his way, and after you have been in the army, your way is different. He sits just behind her, his sword hanging between his knees. He leans forward, resting his hand along the rail, he holds his two gloves lightly. He is absorbed in the ballet. He watches the flying tulle, the madness in the legs, he thinks of the animal garden, where he used to sigh against the eagle's cage, drooping and drawing his breath, of the spotted deer, of the wet and slimy seals, of the quick-nosed otter, of his country, of his men, they war for these things. He moves his spurred heel against his chair, the metal rings, he thinks of sleigh bells, of long untouched acres of snow, when with a start he realizes that the woman with the splendid shoulders has struck him lightly across the cheek. He turns his head slowly, and he says, with his mouth open a little: "And what other objections have you?" You see, he could go on—on to any conclusion, they were already so far along with their history—you see, your father is your history, well, and a good one, a most exceptional one, from one point of view, but where do you begin?

A shot is heard from the other room, and in an instant GART *reels in, he does not see* COSTA *and* JULIE, *or if he does, it does not get his attention.*

GART: It's in there, it's a man's work, we have been left alone too long it's a man's work. It wasn't very light in there, it should have been all right, but it wasn't all right. We have been taught too much devilry. It's his fault, all of it, it all goes back to him, straight back.

He has been too broad. "A woman's hair," he says, "falls between her breasts, she has the odour of connivance about her in a moment. Look at the beasts in the field. He says he was drunk one night in Orange Street and woke up without race prejudice. Observe, he says, that slaughter makes the shoulders rise, and the head descend. See, he says, the little girls stumbling to school, it's their future maternity that makes them stare into the hedges like that. See, he says, how the squirrel lifts its tail, unabashed, unashamed. Regard all the miracles of nature, he tells me, but do not think them sublimely obscure. Observe, he says, these people in high hats bowing to each other, forgetting that they have functions, look at the spectacle of the living swarming with flowers about the dead, don't forget, he says, that the newborn deserve cherishing—

JULIE: *(Who has risen to a sitting posture)* What have you done? Is this your father?

GART: *(Not looking up)* Yes, it was my father, what could you be? What was I thinking of *(He puts his hand across his face)* in there? No, that cannot have been it, there is too much about this place. What could you do? You did everything beautifully, you came unknown and you kept the secret. You were illegal and handsome. You did not know about us.

What could you know? I play the organ. But you do not know what I feel, sitting there on that seat, playing Beethoven like a madman. My father says—but there is pain—

JULIE: *(Going up to him gently)* Your father's hunting pistol?

GART: Yes, but it did not engross me, I could think of other things, I tried, I shot it off, but it was not my sound, I put it down, I was embarrassed—

JULIE: Is this love, Gart?

GART: I don't know, I must think, perhaps, yes, perhaps, but it is no better that way, it makes no conclusions, it does not place anything—

JULIE: What will you do now Gart?

GART: Today I cut my father's hair, over the temples, in the back—that great solid, lewd head under the scissors—a great man, a terrible man—thinks as he pleases, you know—

JULIE: How do you think of that now?

GART: I don't know. That's what is paining me, in here, in my heart. Can nothing make me forget "my father must have his hair cut"? Isn't the thought of death enough to hold the mind, I ramble, I am not arrested, and everything in pain—

JULIE: What shall we do?

GART: Let me lean my head against you. *(He leans his*

head back against her) I wish I did not suffer, I cannot use it, it is all wasted—shameful, shameful.

JULIE: *(Stroking his head)* See, it is nothing, time makes everything nothing, only momentarily, only now, in the meantime as it were, it is painful, but in the end it will be for nothing. Do not be outraged, your mind was one way and your life another. It is stupid and timely to be hurt, it is all a mystery, but that is all it is.

GART: I must abandon you. Must I abandon you? How must I, how shall I?

JULIE: There is the rest of your life, it is how. Do not be frightened that is the great thing. You will in the end, tell your children something—entirely different.

She goes with him to the door, it opens suddenly, GUSTAVA *almost running into the room. She is in great agitation and she darts at* JULIE.

GUSTAVA: There he was, he was going to kill himself, do you understand he was going to kill himself but he didn't, do you understand that, do you know about that? He had despair, well then one kills oneself, isn't that so? He went to his room, that room he was born in, grew up in. He used to go there and look in the mirror, and he saw a face that he understood, what must it have been then when he saw one that he did not know?

JULIE: My dear Gustava—

GUSTAVA: Because he cannot die! You should play with simple natures, natures with one beginning and one end, straight through, like mine, like mine, if you had stopped at me there could have been dignity, you could have counted on *me* to the end.

JULIE: Just what do you mean?

GUSTAVA: He has outwitted you, he has outwitted himself, he has outwitted father, because he has to come to more conclusions than one. I should have known all the time what could torment me and what could not.

JULIE: And what could?

GUSTAVA: Disappointment.

COSTA: *(Trying to get out)* Let me go.

GUSTAVA: *(Throwing him back with all her force)* You stay! Stay where you are. *(Continuing to* JULIE*)* That's all a woman suffers, disappointment.

JULIE: *(Very calmly)* Shall I tell you something?

GUSTAVA: Can you tell anything?

JULIE: *(Ignoring her tone)* I'll tell you a secret, it's a very important one, quite, quite important. I have never been ill, no malady of the heart, no malady of the gorge, no malady of the soul. I have loved many people, but never with a sick love, perhaps that later, but now there is nothing sick in me, that is what you resent, that is natural, I have no belief, as you have in "astounding" evidence. The man becomes sick, very well, he looks at all the faces in history, none appeases him, tenderly he goes over his pain. Here is a suffering comparable to Christ's, here a suffering comparable to Dante, here a wound comparable to a soldier's, here another comparable to a student's, and again a malady comparable to the distemper of an aristocrat, but there is one comparable to none, and this is his. He kills himself, perhaps, just at a quarter after four. They find him in his room, beside him is the photograph of a boxer and a ballet-dancer, it is all one. There is the pistol, in his hand, a brief stillness in existence but is that evidence? I choose to think not.

It might have been at seven, he might have been found laughing to himself with nothing worse inflict-ed on his person than a grimace, there might have been not a single photograph in the room, perhaps this time it was a few copies of a musical journal or medical books on the diseases of horses, a dictionary, he might have looked into the faces of history, and have found in one a madness comparable, a ferocity comparable, a situation as ludicrous, a sensation as mirthful. It is all accident, there is only this at one time, and that at another, and above all, it is not to be judged, but you are young, yes, for you there must be evidence, there must be a conclusion to the drama, or you cannot go on, there must be a cause for an effect, there must be a beginning and an end, yet—see nothing as fixed, certain, it lacks dignity, it is not splendid but it is truth—truth is not splendid you know, because it deals with such poor material—do not try to accomplish destiny, let it accomplish you.

GUSTAVA: This is Julie von Bartmann speaking?

JULIE: This is Julie von Bartmann.

GUSTAVA: It is all a lie! You are making everything pretty, incredibly pretty! You are about to become subtle; courtesy toward destiny—well that embarrasses me, do you understand, embarrasses me—

JULIE: I include that in my destruction. *(Quickly, sharply)* Are all the boys here that I ever loved? Are all the wars over? Who is the match of Julie, and the passion of Julie, and the death of Julie? Why do the dogs bark? You do not know. Why are masses sad in the churches? You cannot answer. When was I first called great and what day shall I begin to be forgotten? You do not know, you cannot know!

At this moment BASIL, *slowly opening the door, appears in the threshold, he stands there, lightly, on the tips of his toes, two fingers of his right hand are thrust into his vest. He is smiling like a child, happily, as one who sees no debacle to his discovery.*

BASIL: Gentlemen, ladies— *(*GUSTAVA, *turning about, opens her mouth to speak. With a slight movement of his head)* No, no, do not say it. *(He looks from one to the other with a bright gaiety)* Do you see me? *(Nothing)* Here I am, a touch of the unknown—the great morass. What is in this man, you say, well, first there is the dark border—one travels painfully here, that is intended; then the second, this is dense, sharp, bristling, trained to be on the watch, like a pack of hounds in the hills, wherever you turn you hear the baying, *(He looks down at himself as a stranger might)* then another, this is the man's upbringing, a carefully disordered stretch, helter, skelter, and all which ways, and then—there is the core, *(He smiles, putting his hands in first one then another of his pockets as if a little puzzled)* the core—

GUSTAVA: Father!

BASIL: No, now it is beyond that, this now is a nameless quality, and what is that quality? That quality is— gentleness—a vast indestructible unalloyed softness. It is terrible because it is so dense and determined. It flows, it boils and it cannot be displaced, it is a quicksand, and that which it gathers it does not give up. You see how it is, not patient, but eternal—

GUSTAVA: Father!

BASIL: And the secret? Shall I, Basil Born, divulge that secret? Is this the moment? There is always a moment, is this it? *(He walks a step into the room, looking up at the rafters as if he had forgotten everything and everyone)* It is the saving miracle, that core, it has been called the heart by some, and by some the soul. That core's secret—inappropriateness—some call it the turning point—

GART: *(In a sick voice)* Stop—

BASIL: You see that child—born defendant and accuser! You do not understand, and yet it is all simple; incredible and not painful at all, not in the least. Yes, Basil tells you all it is peaceful—better, it has come to a noble conclusion. *(He looks joyful)* It has always been this way with me, because I am friends with time, past, present, future. Turn time back, give her a moment for forethought, and where would we be, and what doing? But no, time is a slut, she allows us to exist. Turn her back and you shall see. I have turned her back and mated with her. This is prophesy.

JULIE: *(With irony)* And the masterstroke?

BASIL: No, that I am happy, that's the masterstroke. Ask anything of me, any one of you, anything, I am capable of it. I want to show that I not only can do something splendid, but that I myself can think of something splendid to do, there is a great difference. We are all here, the stage is set, and suddenly, appropriately, I walk in. Now Basil, be enormous! *(COSTA breaks into a harsh laugh, and is silent again)* They laugh! My own children laugh, they ask nothing of me, are they then incapable? But wait, I'll ask alms of myself, I will pilfer my own life. Leave myself indebted to myself, set myself a splendid beggary! Miracles force themselves upon us, am I the man to keep them waiting? I have not welcomed you, well, now I appear before you, at the critical moment you might say, now I acclaim you. Julie von Bartmann, the multitude bow down to you, you having whipped them into submission with your voice. I have not heard that voice, yet I bow down to you, for do I not stand in the presence of the very sheath of that magic? This is Julie, the magnificent Julie, there is nothing like her in the world! She does not understand yet, she does not see where all this fit in. She is worldly, oh, in the highest, the very highest sense. She will understand later, later, when everyone else has quite forgotten, that is the way one becomes possessed of beauty, religion even—thinking of a thing hundreds have forgotten. *(Not unaware of the amazement and displeasure of the children)* Well, when I was a boy, I used to harp on a few truths most incessantly, such as: "Honor knows no alternative," or: "The way of the strong is a long and narrow way, one may not turn aside." But now I come to kiss this hand. You will accept that kiss, the kiss of the mystery that becomes the parable, acknowledging my mind's narrow ring, and so ascend—(*During this speech, drawing himself up in his joy, his excitement, his eloquence and his fervour, he slips, tries to right himself, fails, and falling on all fours, head lowered, is silent for a long moment*) And yet—I would have honored you like a man. Well, it has become simpler still—the acknowledgement of the beast. Accept it, Julie von Bartmann—The Beast salutes you!

GUSTAVA: (*Quietly, almost dully, to* JULIE) Go, go, it is all over. You see what he has managed—accomplished. Go, go, take everything and go. You see yourself—we are reunited—we need nothing—it is all finished—settled—

JULIE: (*After a moment's silence—going toward the door—with admiration*) Immense! Immense! (*She goes out*)

Curtain.

Cagnes sur Mer, Alpes Maritimes, France
November 1923 – April 1924

Made in the USA
Middletown, DE
19 March 2022